The Seven Continents
Asia

JOHN SON

Children's Press®
An Imprint of Scholastic Inc.

Content Consultant

Jing Sun, Ph.D., Associate Professor of Political Science, University of Denver

Library of Congress Cataloging-in-Publication Data
Names: Son, John., author.
Title: Asia / by John Son.
Description: New York, NY : Children's Press, an imprint of Scholastic Inc., [2019] I Series: A true book I
    Includes bibliographical references and index.
Identifiers: LCCN 2018026110l ISBN 9780531128060 (library binding) I ISBN 9780531134146 (pbk.)
Subjects: LCSH: Asia—Juvenile literature.
Classification: LCC DS5 .S585 2019 I DDC 950—dc23
LC record available at https://lccn.loc.gov/2018026110

All rights reserved. Published in 2019 by Children's Press, an imprint of Scholastic Inc.
Printed in North Mankato, MN, USA 113

SCHOLASTIC, CHILDREN'S PRESS, A TRUE BOOK™, and associated logos are trademarks and/or
registered trademarks of Scholastic Inc.

Scholastic Inc., 557 Broadway, New York, NY 10012

1 2 3 4 5 6 7 8 9 10 R 28 27 26 25 24 23 22 21 20 19

Front: Asia
Back: Floating market in Vietnam

Find the Truth!

Everything you are about to read is true *except* for one of the sentences on this page.

Which one is **TRUE**?

T or F   Asia has more mountains than any other continent.

T or F   Red pandas are plentiful throughout Asia.

Find the answers in this book.

3

Contents

THE BIG TRUTH!

Pollution in Asia

Rollerblading through
smog in China

4

The holy city of Varanasi in India

Giant panda

Greenland

Alaska

North Pole

ARCTIC OCEAN

Arctic Circle

PA
O

Siberia

RUSSIA

*Sea
of
Okhotsk*

Sakhalin

Ob River

Yenisei River

Lena River

EUROPE

L. Baikal

GEORGIA

KAZAKHSTAN

Aral Sea

L. Balkash

MONGOLIA

NORTH
KOREA

TURKEY

Caspian Sea

Black Sea

ARMENIA

UZBEKISTAN

Beijing

Sea
of
Japa
(Eas
Sea

CYPRUS

SYRIA

TURKMENISTAN

KYRGYZSTAN

SOUT
KORE

LEBANON

*Huang He
(Yellow River)*

ISRAEL

IRAQ

AZERBAIJAN

TAJIKISTAN

Tigris R.

JORDAN

AFGHANISTAN

*Chaing Jiang
(Yangtze River)*

Euphrates R.

Tibet

CHINA

TA

*Red
Sea*

KUWAIT

BAHRAIN

Indus R.

NEPAL

BHUTAN

QATAR

PAKISTAN

PHI

SAUDI
ARABIA

U.A.E.

New Delhi

Ganges River

BANGLADESH

MYANMAR

LAOS

*South
China
Sea*

OMAN

*Hainan I.
(China)* Manila

YEMEN

INDIA

Arabian Sea

THAILAND

VIETNAM

N

*Bay of
Bengal*

BRUNEI

AFRICA

W   E

MALDIVES

*Andaman
& Nicobar
Is.
(India)*

CAMBODIA

MALAYSIA

S

SINGAPORE

Equator

0   300 MI

SRI LANKA

0   500 KM

INDONESIA*

INDIAN OCEAN

AUS

Indonesia extends off the eastern edge of this map. The country can be seen in full on the Australia/Oceania map.

Continent Close-up

Asia is the biggest continent.

It contains about one-third of all the land on Earth. It is also the most populous continent, with almost four and a half billion people. This is more than 60 percent of Earth's total population! The people of Asia represent an incredibly diverse range of cultures, and they live in a wide variety of environments.

Kazakhstan

Land area	About 17,226,200 square miles (44,614,000 sq km)
Number of independent countries	About 50
Estimated population (2018)	About 4.5 billion
Main languages	Mandarin, Hindi, Arabic
Largest country	Russia
Smallest country	Maldives
Fast fact	China and India are the only countries in the world with populations above one billion.

China

More than 1,500 islands make up Raja Ampat.

Indonesia's Raja Ampat Islands are located just off the coast of New Guinea.

CHAPTER 1

Land and Climate

Asia shares part of its border with the continents of Europe and Africa. From north to south, it stretches from the Arctic Circle to the tropics south of the equator. From east to west, it stretches from the Pacific Ocean to the Mediterranean Sea. Because of its great size, the continent is often divided into six smaller regions: central Asia, northern Asia, eastern Asia, Southeast Asia, southern Asia, and the Middle East.

Indonesia's Mount Agung volcano has erupted as recently as 2018.

A Varied Landscape

Asia's sprawling landscape contains a wide variety of environments. It is home to barren deserts, tropical islands, and rugged mountain ranges. It also hosts frozen tundras and lush rain forests. Some of the world's coldest and hottest places are located in Asia. The tallest and lowest places on Earth's surface are found on the continent. So are some of the world's most crowded cities and most deserted areas.

Towering Peaks

The Himalayas, a mountain range that runs along the border between Nepal and China, contain many of the tallest mountains in the world. The tallest

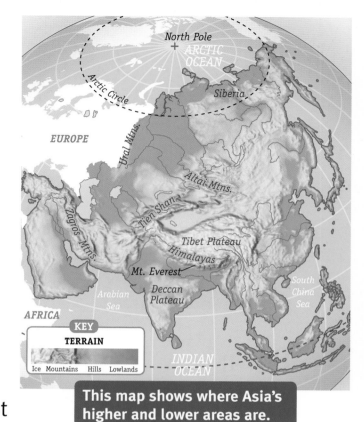

This map shows where Asia's higher and lower areas are.

of all is Mount Everest, which peaks at 29,035 feet (8,850 meters). That's almost as tall as 20 Empire State Buildings! To give the human body enough time to adjust to the extreme elevation, it takes 40 days to climb Mount Everest safely. Only about half of the people who try to climb the mountain reach the summit successfully.

You can read a book while floating in the Dead Sea.

The water in the Dead Sea is about 10 times saltier than ocean water.

Down Low

Asia is also home to the lowest place on land. The Dead Sea is a saltwater lake between Israel and Jordan. Its shores lie about 1,410 feet (430 m) below sea level. Because the lake is about 10 times saltier than the ocean, no animal can survive in its waters. Only a few species of bacteria and algae live in this unusual environment. But the saltiness also makes it very easy for people to float on the lake's surface.

Let It Flow

Some of the world's most incredible rivers run through Asia. At a length of 3,915 miles (6,300 kilometers), China's Yangtze River is the longest river in Asia. Many people make a living fishing its waters. Asia's waterways have always been vital to the **economies** of its various peoples. They provide water to **irrigate** the surrounding lands. Many rivers, such as the Indus River in southern Asia, were vital to the development of early civilizations.

Many people believe the waters of the Ganges River can cure illnesses and purify the spirit.

The famous Ganges River flows through India and Bangladesh.

Buses travel down a flooded street in Dhaka, Bangladesh.

RECORD TEMPERATURES

HIGHEST	LOWEST
Tirat Tsvi, Israel; June 21, 1942	Verkhoyansk, Russia, February 5 and 7, 1892, and again in Oimekon, Russia; February 6, 1933
129°F 53.9°C	**−90°F** −67.8°C

Let's Talk About the Weather

Asia's climate is the most extreme in the world. Only a small part of the continent has the right climate to support crop growth. In Southeast Asia, the summer monsoon season brings heavy rains and flooding. In the far northern part of Russia called Siberia, it is freezing cold year-round. Other areas, such as western Asia, are extremely dry, with very little rainfall. But no matter the climate, Asia's people have found ways to build communities.

The World's Most Perfect Volcano

Located in the Philippines, Mount Mayon has erupted more than 40 times in the past 500 years. The most recent eruption was in 2018, when lava shot 2,300 feet (701 m) above the volcano's crater. The **symmetry** of its shape makes it the world's most perfect volcanic cone. Despite its constant activity, the volcano's natural beauty makes it a popular destination for climbers and campers. When the volcano is calm, it is possible to reach the crater in two or three days.

Mount Mayon is one of many active volcanoes in the Philippines.

There are only about 1,800 giant pandas left in the wild today.

The giant panda is found only in China.

Plants and Animals

Many types of **biomes** can be found in Asia's six regions. Some are dry and hot, while some are high and rocky. Others are freezing cold or damp and humid with year-round rain. Each biome is home to its own family of plants, animals, and insects. Giant pandas, red pandas, orangutans, and komodo dragons are just a few of the animals unique to the Asian continent.

Deep in the Rain Forests

Much of Southeast Asia is covered in rain forests. Year-round rainfall creates an ideal environment for some of the most diverse plant and animal life in the world. Animals such as the Bengal tiger, slender loris, orangutan, and king cobra are found only in the rain forests of Southeast Asia. The tallest tree in Asia's forests is the tualang tree, which can reach heights of up to 280 feet (85 m). Its high branches are the perfect place for giant honeybees to build their honeycombs out of reach of bears.

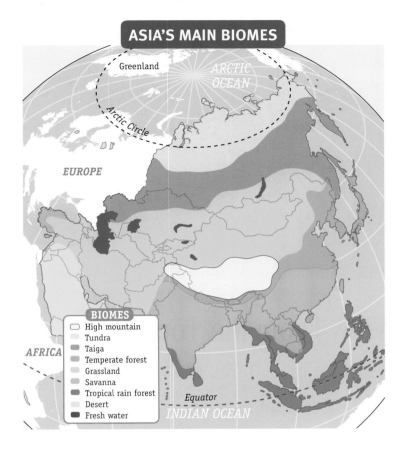

Greenland

ARCTIC OCEAN

Arctic Circle

EUROPE

AFRICA

Equator

INDIAN OCEAN

BIOMES
- High mountain
- Tundra
- Taiga
- Temperate forest
- Grassland
- Savanna
- Tropical rain forest
- Desert
- Fresh water

A Disappearing Biome

The rain forests of Southeast Asia are the oldest rain forests on Earth. Unfortunately, **deforestation** has wiped out thousands of plant and animal species. However, environmental activists have influenced some of Asia's governments to protect the forests that remain.

The View From the Top

Asia has more mountains than any other continent. Dozens of mountain ranges stretch across its landmass. The towering Himalayas separate the Indian subcontinent from the rest of Asia. The Kunlun mountain range is one of the longest in Asia. It stretches across western China for over 1,850 miles (2,977 km). Another significant range is the Zagros Mountains, located in Iran and Iraq. Asia's mountains are home to animals such as snow leopards, falcons, and eagles.

Barren Deserts

Deserts are another major biome found in Asia. The largest is the Gobi Desert in Mongolia and China. Its name means "place without water" in Mongolian. The Rub al-Khali is a desert located on the Arabian **Peninsula**. It covers about 25 percent of Saudi Arabia. Very little plant life exists in Asia's deserts, but many animals survive the harsh conditions. Among them are jerboas, pit vipers, and owls.

The name *Gobi* is simply the Mongolian word for "desert."

A Frozen Landscape

Siberia covers most of northern Asia and has very few human residents. This is due to the extremely cold and snowy weather year-round. Much of Siberia is made up of a type of treeless and frozen biome called tundra. Lichens, mosses, and short grasses are the main plants that survive in this freezing environment. Reindeer, lemmings, and polar bears thrive in the tundra.

Reindeer noses are designed to warm the air before it reaches their lungs.

Endangered in Asia

Many of Asia's plant and animal species are in danger of dying out, usually due to human activities. Here are just a few:

Orangutan

Home: Sumatra and Borneo

Orangutans' forest homes are being rapidly destroyed by logging and farming. They are also captured illegally to be sold as pets.

Red Panda

Home: Eastern Himalayas

Global warming is forcing the tree-loving red panda out of its protected habitats. This animal is also being **poached** for its beautiful fur.

Bengal Tiger

Home: India

These powerful cats are often poached for their unique striped fur.

Javan Rhinoceros

Home: Java

Poaching has nearly destroyed the Javan rhinoceros population. Javan rhinos were once the most common rhino species in Asia. In 2017, only 67 of these animals remained. They are protected in Java's Ujung Kulon National Park.

Pollution in Asia

Over the past few decades, Asia has become the manufacturing center of the world. Automobiles, computers, and clothes are just a few of the many products that come out of Asia. A great deal of oil and coal are also extracted from the continent. As a result of this rapid industrialization, Asia has developed major pollution problems. In China, most rivers and lakes are badly polluted. Many of Asia's biggest cities are among the most polluted in the world.

Many people in Asia wear masks to filter out pollution as they breathe.

Leading the Charge

To address these problems with pollution, many Asian countries are raising public awareness of climate change and promoting clean energy technologies. For example, India and China produce a great deal of solar energy. This cuts down on the use of harmful fossil fuels. In countries such as Indonesia, paper companies are promising to protect forests to help make up for the trees they harvest. Many Asian cities are also converting to electric taxis to decrease air pollution.

Pollution Sources

- Burning fossil fuels
- Farms
- Toxic waste from factories
- Trash
- Deforestation

Ways People Can Help

- Use **renewable energy** sources
- Recycle
- Walk or ride a bike instead of driving
- Plant a tree
- Use less water

The Great Ziggurat at Ur was the most famous ziggurat in Mesopotamia.

The ruins of 30 ziggurats still exist in Asia.

CHAPTER 3

A Peek at the Past

Thousands of years ago, some of the world's earliest civilizations developed in Asia. They rose up near fertile valleys along the banks of the Tigris, Euphrates, Indus, and Yellow rivers, where people could grow crops and raise animals. In these locations, small settlements grew into towns and cities. Within these cities, complex societies formed. Trade between cities helped expand the civilizations even further.

The Cradle of Civilization

Mesopotamia, the world's first civilization, emerged between the Tigris and Euphrates rivers about 5,000 years ago. Today, this area is made up of Iraq and parts of Syria and Turkey. The Mesopotamians learned to divert water from the rivers to their crops. This allowed them to develop agriculture. The rise of agriculture led to other new technologies, including metalworking and the invention of the wheel.

The ancient Mesopotamian city of Nimrud was built along the banks of the Tigris River.

This ancient cuneiform tablet was used to keep track of accounts.

A Way to Write

Invented by the Mesopotamians, cuneiform (KYOO-nih-form) is one of the world's earliest writing systems. Characters were written by pressing a reed **stylus** into wet clay. Thousands of cuneiform tablets have been discovered. They include letters, heroic tales, poems, and even receipts for goods. It took about 200 years for modern scholars to understand the cuneiform writing system. Now they can read the words people wrote down thousands of years ago.

The Indus Valley Civilization

The second major ancient Asian civilization arose around the Indus River in present-day Pakistan and northwestern India in about 2500 BCE. Called the Harappans, these people developed an advanced city life with planned streets and elaborate buildings. Their homes even had bathrooms, and they placed trash bins along their wide city streets.

Timeline of Asian History

3500 BCE
The wheel is invented in Mesopotamia.

550 BCE
Cyrus the Great founds the Persian Empire.

| 3500 BCE | 2200 BCE | 550 BCE | 130 BCE |

2200 BCE
The Xia Dynasty rules in an area around the Yellow River basin. It is the oldest known dynasty in China.

130 BCE
The Silk Road opens trade throughout Asia.

Early Chinese Civilization

Groups of primitive villages clustered on the banks of the Yellow River as far back as 5000 BCE. Over time, these villages grew to become the civilization we now know as China. Beginning in about 1600 BCE, the Shang **dynasty** ruled China for almost 500 years. Its people were skilled at weaving silk and working with bronze. They also developed China's first writing system.

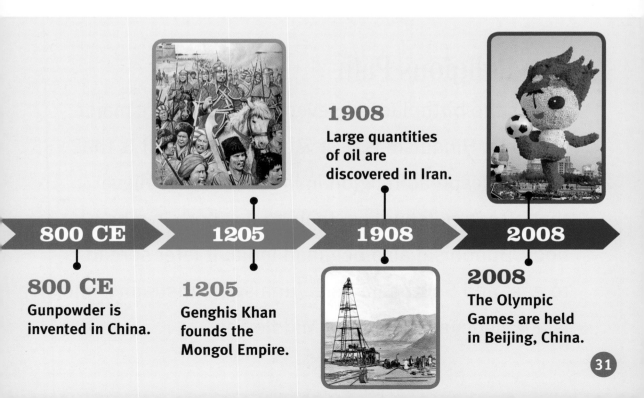

1908
Large quantities of oil are discovered in Iran.

800 CE ▷ **1205** ▷ **1908** ▷ **2008**

800 CE
Gunpowder is invented in China.

1205
Genghis Khan founds the Mongol Empire.

2008
The Olympic Games are held in Beijing, China.

In 2001, the Taliban destroyed the world's tallest Buddha statues in Afghanistan. In 2015, the ancient statues were temporarily brought back to life by 3D light projections.

The Religious Path

Asia is the birthplace of several of the world's major religions. Hinduism is over 4,000 years old. It is the most widespread religion in India. Hindus believe that after a person dies, their soul is born in a new body. Buddhism also began in India. It later spread to east and Southeast Asia. Judaism, Christianity, and Islam all developed in the Middle East.

Martial Arts of Asia

Asian martial arts were developed as a form of exercise and self-defense by monks in India and Tibet. Once the techniques spread to the rest of Asia, different people developed their own styles, techniques, and philosophies. For example, kung fu arose in China, while Japan developed a style called karate. Almost all types of martial arts are based on using different parts of the body for self-defense. Today, many people around the world take martial arts classes for exercise and to build self-confidence.

Martial arts students practice kung fu in China's Jiangxi Province.

Shanghai, China, has a population of 24 million people.

At a height of 1,535 feet (468 m), the Oriental Pearl Tower is one of the tallest structures in Shanghai.

Asia Today

Today, Asia is changing at a dizzying pace. In the past several decades, Japan, South Korea, Taiwan, Hong Kong, Singapore, Southeast Asia, and China have experienced major economic booms. And the rest of Asia is starting to catch up to them. Electronics, clothes, cars, and oil are some of the goods Asia supplies to the rest of the world. The skylines of Asia's cities have been transformed by some of the world's tallest buildings. But though there is great wealth, there is also great poverty. More than 70 percent of the world's malnourished children live in Asia.

A Crowded Continent

Asia is the largest continent not just in area but also by population. Several of the largest cities in the world are located in Asia. Experts estimate that in the near future, most of Asia's population will be crowded into these rapidly expanding cities. However, the Arabian Desert and Tibetan Plateau are some of the least populated areas on the planet. Asia is also home to many diverse ethnic groups. The continent's people can have many different skin tones, facial features, and other traits.

Shibuya Crossing in Tokyo, Japan, is believed to be the world's busiest crosswalk.

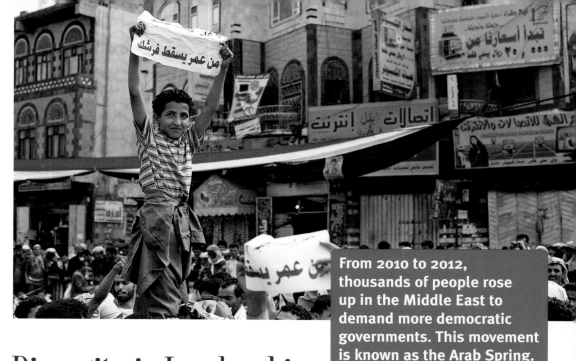

From 2010 to 2012, thousands of people rose up in the Middle East to demand more democratic governments. This movement is known as the Arab Spring.

Diversity in Leadership

There are many different types of governments in Asia. Some countries, like Saudi Arabia, are monarchies. This means they are led by kings who are born into a royal family. Many Asian countries are democracies, where government officials are elected by the country's citizens. Some democratic nations, such as Japan and Thailand, have monarchies too. However, their royal leaders do not have much real power in government.

Asian Pop

Asian pop culture has developed a highly visible presence around the world. In the 1970s, Hong Kong brought action-packed kung fu films to international cinemas. Japanese comics and animation have a major global following. Films from countries such as China, Thailand, India, and Iran have millions of fans and win many awards. K-pop is a form of popular music from South Korea. Its biggest music videos have hundreds of millions of views on YouTube.

The music video for the K-pop song "Gangnam Style" by Psy was the first YouTube video to receive a billion views.

Made in Asia

Many goods are manufactured in Asia and exported to the rest of the world. Oil is the main export from Middle Eastern countries such as Saudi Arabia, Iran, and Kuwait. Japan and South Korea are major exporters of automobiles. Electronic devices such as cell phones, computers, and televisions are manufactured in east Asian countries. China is also a major exporter of toys and steel. In addition, south and Southeast Asian countries make much of the clothing worn by most of the world.

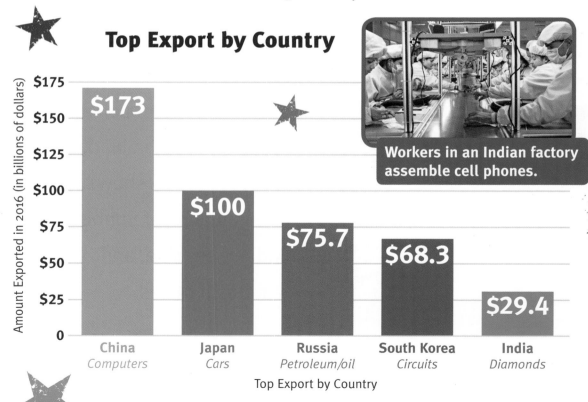

Top Export by Country

Workers in an Indian factory assemble cell phones.

Amount Exported in 2016 (in billions of dollars)

Country	Amount
China — Computers	$173
Japan — Cars	$100
Russia — Petroleum/oil	$75.7
South Korea — Circuits	$68.3
India — Diamonds	$29.4

Top Export by Country

Source: MIT Observatory of Economic Complexity

Delicious Dishes

Asia's cultural diversity is reflected deliciously in its cuisine. Rice is the main staple of many Asian countries. Tofu is unique to east and south Asia, while curry flavors the foods of India, Bangladesh, and Pakistan. Chickpeas, dates, and honey are common in Middle Eastern recipes. Japan has brought sushi to the rest of the world. Fish sauce and lemongrass are common ingredients in the dishes of Southeast Asian countries such as Vietnam and Thailand. Filipino cuisine shows the influence of Spanish, Indian, Chinese, and American tastes.

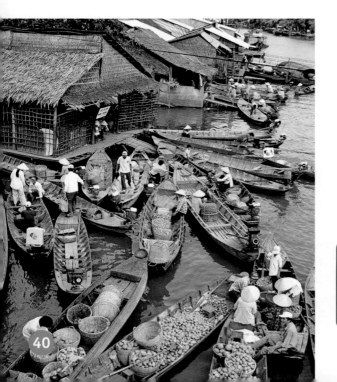

In Vietnam, vendors in boats sometimes gather to form "floating markets."

At the Taiwan Lantern Festival, thousands of paper lanterns are lit and sent floating up to the sky, celebrating the end of the Lunar New Year.

Celebrate Asia

The people of Asia have many celebrations that go back hundreds, if not thousands, of years. The Lunar New Year is celebrated in east Asian countries such as China, Vietnam, and Singapore. Hindus celebrate the festival known as Holi. People participate by smearing each other with colored powder while dancing wildly in the streets.

Asia is a remarkable place with a rich culture and history. Its influence is felt all around the world. ★

Destination

China

The construction of this 13,000-mile-long (20,921 km) wall began in the 3rd century BCE. The wall was built to defend the Chinese border against invaders and is one of the most recognizable structures in Asia.

TAJ MAHAL
India

One of the most beautiful monuments in the world is the Taj Mahal in India. Built out of white marble, it was completed in 1648 as a tomb for the favorite wife of the Shah Jahan.

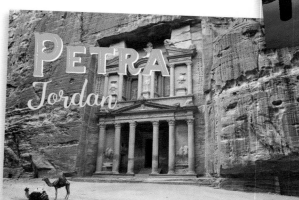

PETRA
Jordan

This ancient city is almost 2,500 years old. The buildings that remain include a theater, temples, and tombs that were all carved out of solid rock.

Asia

Mount Fuji
Japan

Located near the city of Tokyo, this volcano is the tallest mountain in Japan. It is a major symbol in the country's artwork and culture.

Angkor Wat
Cambodia

The ruins of this ancient city in Cambodia are famous for their stunning temples. It is the largest religious monument in the world.

Lake Baikal
Russia

Lake Baikal is the largest freshwater lake in Asia and the deepest lake in the world. It is frozen from December to May and home to the Baikal seal, which is not found anywhere else in the world.

United Arab Emirates
Burj Khalifa

This towering skyscraper in the city of Dubai stands 2,722 feet (830 m) tall, making it the tallest building in the world.

Size: About 17,226,200 square miles (44,614,000 sq km)

Population of Chongqing, China, the continent's most populous city: More than 30 million

Average life expectancy (selected countries): Japan, 84; South Korea, 82; Kuwait, 77; Iran, 74; Philippines, 69; Yemen, 65; Cambodia, 64

Total internet users (selected countries), as of 2016: China, 731 million; India, 374 million; Japan, 116 million; Vietnam, 49 million; Bangladesh, 28 million; Sri Lanka, 7 million; Syria, 5 million

Did you find the truth?

T Asia has more mountains than any other continent.

F Red pandas are plentiful throughout Asia.

Resources

Books

Ganeri, Anita. *Introducing Asia*. Chicago: Heinemann Library, 2014.

Hirsch, Rebecca E. *Asia*. New York: Children's Press, 2012.

Oachs, Emily Rose. *Asia*. Minneapolis: Bellwether Media, 2016.

Onsgard, Bethany. *Asia*. Minneapolis: ABDO Publishing Company, 2014.

Yomtov, Nel. *China*. New York: Children's Press, 2018.

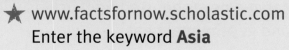

Visit this Scholastic website for more information on Asia:

★ www.factsfornow.scholastic.com
Enter the keyword **Asia**

Important Words

biomes (BYE-ohmz) communities of plants and animals that have common characteristics suited for the environment where they exist

deforestation (dee-for-ih-STAY-shuhn) the removal or cutting down of trees

dynasty (DYE-nuh-stee) a series of rulers belonging to the same family

economies (ih-KAH-nuh-meez) systems of buying, selling, making things, and managing money in a place

irrigate (IR-uh-gate) to supply water to crops by artificial means, such as channels and pipes

peninsula (puh-NIN-suh-luh) a piece of land that sticks out from a larger landmass and is almost completely surrounded by water

poached (POHCHT) hunted or fished illegally on someone else's property

renewable energy (rih-NOO-uh-buhl EN-ur-jee) power from sources that can never be used up, such as wind, tides, sunlight, and geothermal heat

stylus (STYE-luhs) a small instrument that you use like a pen to write

symmetry (SIM-ih-tree) a balanced arrangement of parts on either side of a line or around a central point

Index

Page numbers in **bold** indicate illustrations.

About the Author

John Son is the author of *Finding My Hat*, an NYPL Best Book for the Teen Age about his adventures growing up in Texas as a Korean American; *Relaxation and Yoga* (True Books); and *If You Were a Kid on the Mayflower*. He lives with his family in Brooklyn, New York.